The Happy Humpback Whale

Tales from Tim Faulkner

Illustrated by Elin Matilda Andersson

Deep down in the Antarctic
a happy humpback is eating krill.
Filtering them from the water,
it takes tonnes to have her fill.

Off the ice and into the water,
penguins and seals go diving by.
Above she spots albatrosses
as they glide through the sky.

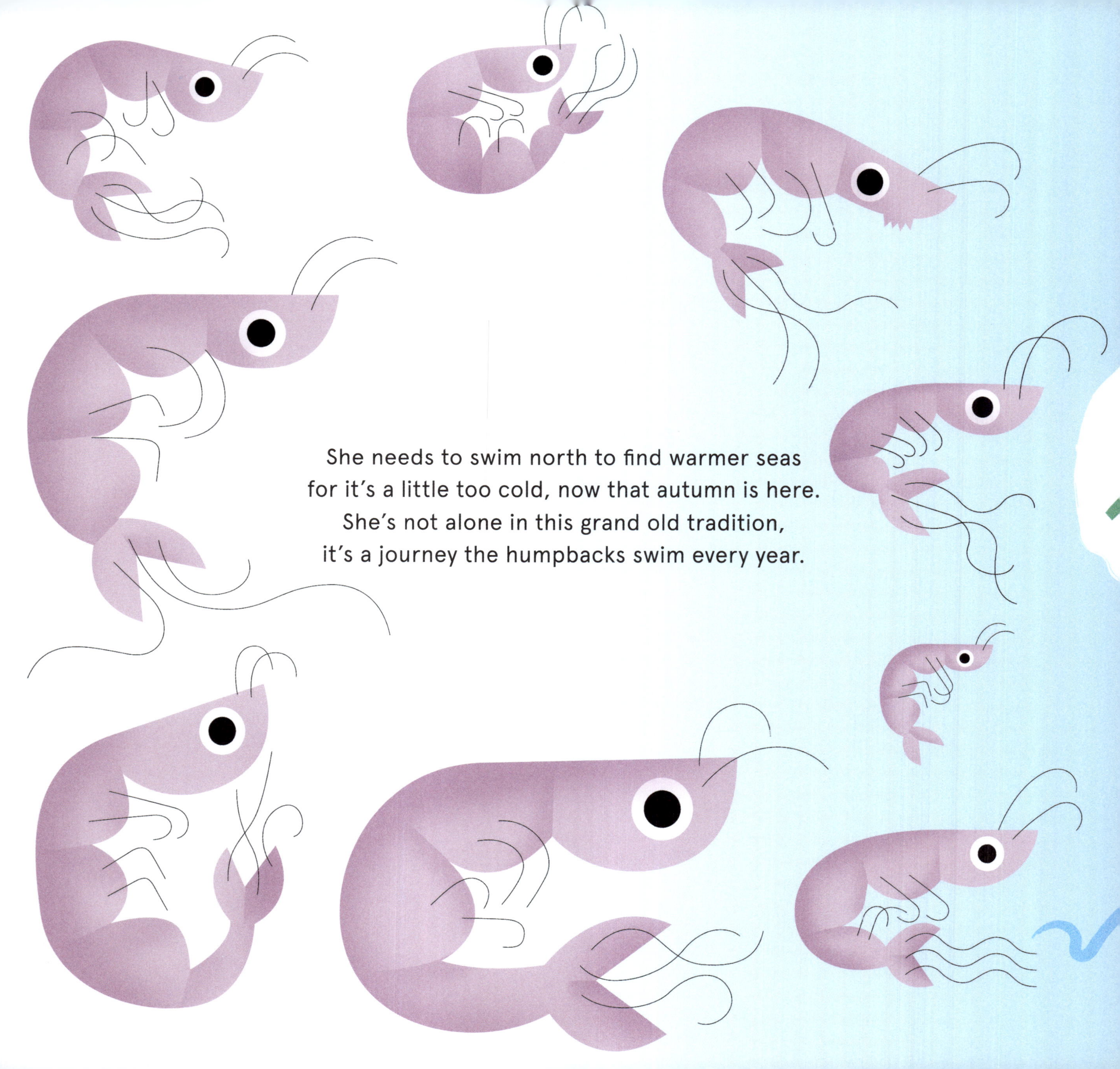

She needs to swim north to find warmer seas
for it's a little too cold, now that autumn is here.
She's not alone in this grand old tradition,
it's a journey the humpbacks swim every year.

The sea is angry and rough
and the wind starts to blow.
The whales group in pods,
and now it's time to go.

They take to the ocean
and make their first sighting of land.
It's Tassie, and they see devils, wombats
and endless beaches of sand.

They pop up again near old Twofold Bay,
a place that the whales used to find scary.
They remember spears and boats filled with men,
it's been over for years, and the whales are less wary.

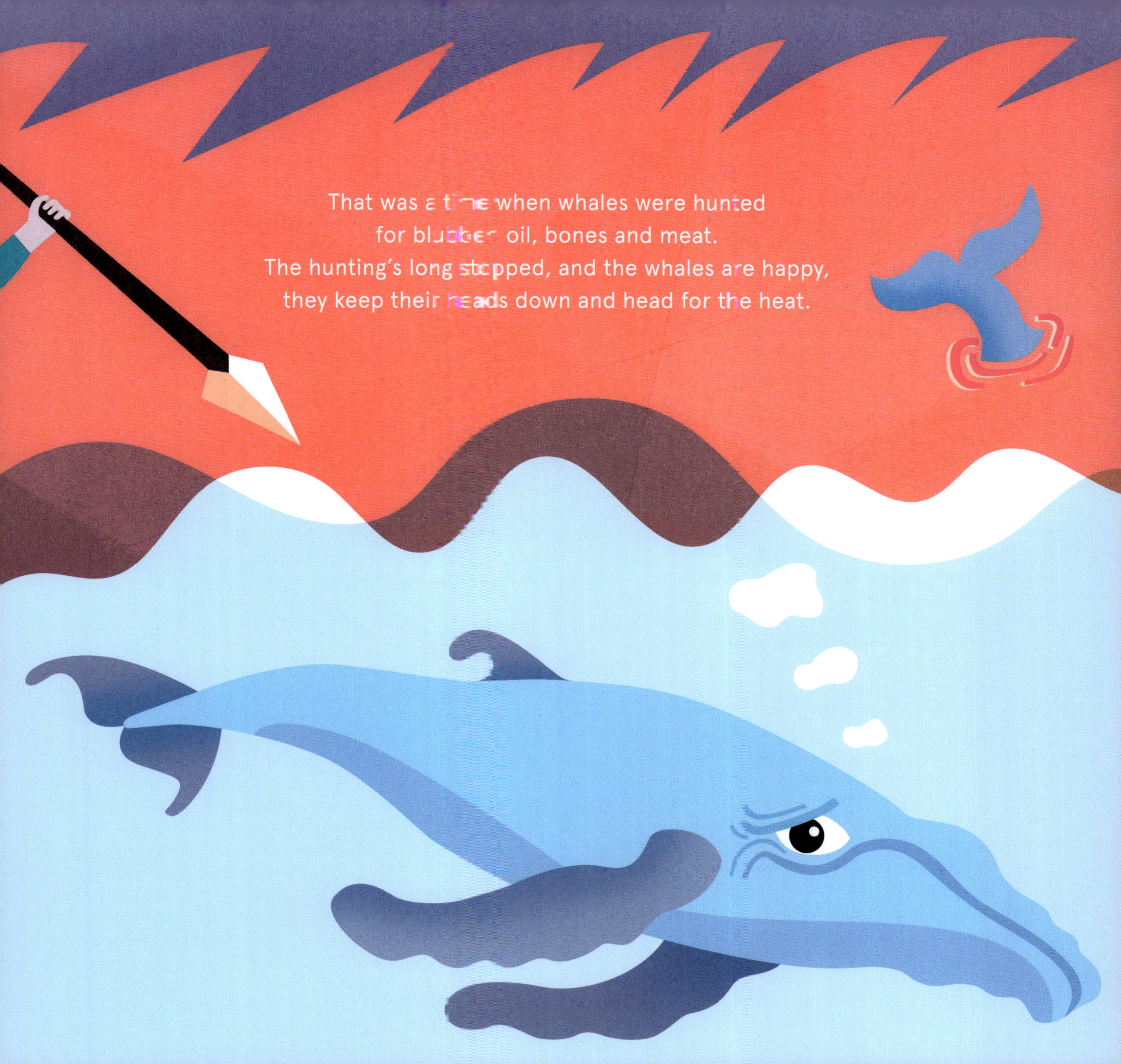
That was a time when whales were hunted
for blubber oil, bones and meat.
The hunting's long stopped, and the whales are happy,
they keep their heads down and head for the heat.

She's reached the warm northern waters
with just enough time, now that winter is here.
She's not alone in this grand old tradition,
it's a journey the humpbacks swim every year.

She stays close to the shore
to avoid any danger,
and passes a Fraser Island dingo
who says, “G’day stranger!”

Looming up ahead
is the Great Barrier Reef.
She spots corals, clownfish, eels
and even bright fish with teeth!

The North Queensland waters are warm
and something magical takes place.
She gives birth to little humpback twins
and names them Harry and Grace.

She swims below to keep them afloat,
and feeds them thick milk to make them both strong.
They sing to one another in their deep, low voices
a complex, beautiful and melodious song.

It's time to move on and the whales all turn south,
the water's quite warm, now that springtime is here.
They're not alone in this grand old tradition,
it's a journey the humpbacks swim every year.

She breaches and splashes down
and takes a breath in-between.
They're all swimming south again
and she can't believe what she's seen.

The Opera House, the Harbour Bridge
and rugged sandstone cliffs.
"That surely must be Sydney,"
a passing dolphin insists.

Further down in Bass Strait
there's something in the water;
a great white shark is circling round
and snaps the whales into order.

The pod gets in formation
and they slap their tails hard.
They move fast, the shark is gone
and they can drop their guard.

The whale and her family are nearly back home
to their krill-filled icy waters, now that summer is here.
They're not alone in this grand old tradition,
it's a journey the humpbacks swim every year.

It has been months and months
since Mumma whale has eaten.
With the twins drinking milk daily,
Mum is starting to feel beaten.

But now they eat and they rest,
and play around in the icy, blue sea.
They're back home in the Antarctic,
this happy humpback family of three.

Find a spot along the coast
and you might see them go forth,
in autumn or springtime
as they swim south and north.

To see a whale swimming by,
one of the largest creatures of all,
is something that you'll never forget
whether you're grown up or you're small.

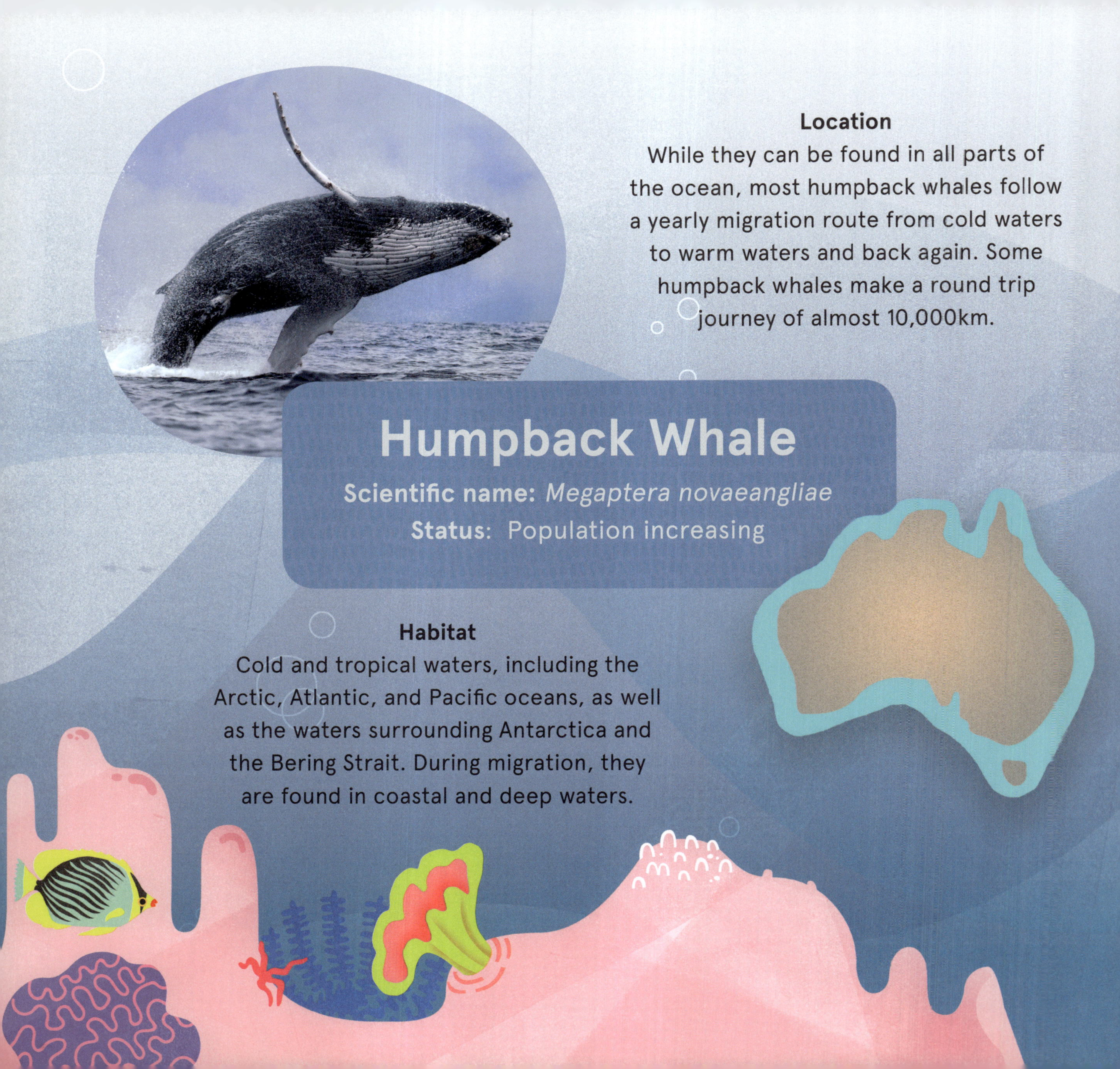

Humpback Whale

Scientific name: *Megaptera novaeangliae*

Status: Population increasing

Location

While they can be found in all parts of the ocean, most humpback whales follow a yearly migration route from cold waters to warm waters and back again. Some humpback whales make a round trip journey of almost 10,000km.

Habitat

Cold and tropical waters, including the Arctic, Atlantic, and Pacific oceans, as well as the waters surrounding Antarctica and the Bering Strait. During migration, they are found in coastal and deep waters.

Appearance

They have a small, pointed dorsal fin and grooves on their throat. They're often covered in barnacles and short, coarse hair. Adults are 12-16m long and weigh about 36,000kg – almost the size of a bus!

Life cycle

Breeding occurs mostly in winter to early spring, in warm tropical waters. Each female typically bears a single calf every 2-3 years and the gestation period is 12 months. Their life expectancy is 45-50 years.

Diet

They feed on krill and small fish and eat up to 1.5 tonnes of food a day. During feeding, large volumes of water and food are taken into the mouth, the water is filtered through baleen plates and the food is trapped inside.

Good senses

They have excellent hearing, especially at low frequencies, which is valuable in the dark ocean environment where their vision is impaired. They can dive for up to 30 minutes, but usually last only up to 15 minutes, to a depth of 150-210m.

Saving the whales

Humpback whales were targeted by whalers throughout the 19th century. The International Whaling Commission gave them worldwide protection status in 1966 and populations have doubled in the last 10 years.

Vocalisation

Humpback whales are the noisiest and most imaginative whales when it comes to songs. They have long, varied, complex, eerie, beautiful songs that include recognisable sequences of sounds.

Social groups

They travel in large, temporary groups. The strongest and most lasting bonds are between a mother and calf.

Predators

Humpback whales have very few natural predators. Their only other predators, besides humans, are sharks and killer whales, who feed on the sick, injured or young.

Tim Faulkner

Wrestling a saltwater crocodile, wrangling a deadly taipan and milking a funnel-web spider is all in a day's work for Tim Faulkner! He could do all that and still find time to release a blue-tongue lizard, tag a wild platypus and save the Tasmanian devil from extinction!

Tim is the Director and Head of Conservation at the Australian Reptile Park in Somersby, NSW, and The Devil Ark at Barrington Tops, NSW. Australian Geographic Conservationist of the Year (2015), Tim features in numerous TV shows, including his own **Wild Life of Tim Faulkner**, showcasing Australian wildlife to the world.

Tim developed a love for the Australian bush and wildlife at a young age. He is proud to be sharing these stories with children, with the hope they will feel the same love for native creatures.

The Happy Humpback Whale

First edition published by Australian Geographic in 2017
An imprint of Bauer Media Ltd
54 Park Street, Sydney, NSW 2000
Telephone +61 2 9263 9813
Email editorial@ausgeo.com.au
www.ausgeo.com.au

Australian Geographic customer service
1300 555 176 from within Australia (local call rate)
+61 2 8667 5295 from outside Australia

Author: Tim Faulkner
Illustrator: Elin Matilda Andersson
Designer: Mike Rossi
Art director: Mike Ellott
Editor: Lauren Smith
Proof reader: Erin Mayo

CEO: Nick Chan
Publisher: Jo Runciman
Australian Geographic editor-in-chief: Chrissie Goldrick

A portion of the funds from the sale of this book go to support the Australian Geographic Society, a not-for-profit organisation dedicated to sponsoring conservation, scientific research, adventures and expeditions.